WHY DO THEY HATE US . IMMIGRATION GUIDE TO ITALY

Immigration, has given the European nations the serious problem of solving the acceptance and the integration of the newcomers into their nations.

How to balance the necessary opening of the borders with the interests of their own citizens who might
feel threatened in their primary needs (for example they think about the lack of work places).
It is with this in mind, and in general to ask the question WHY DO THEY HATE US ?

In these pages, every non EU member can find -synthesized and simplified - the principle laws necessary to live in these countries taking Italy as an example people are worried about foreigners stealing their places of work,and the insurgency of different crimes that comes with immigrant due to lack of ingnorance of their Host country laws.

A kind of which one can refer in order to know immediately the correct way to behave; what to do or what not to do, what to expect from the public authorities and who to turn to; what his rights and his obligations, are what constitutes a crime in Italy, what procedure to take in order to legalize his status, and so on.

I hope i have produced something useful for both the foreigners who often violate the laws due to ignorance and lack of understanding, and for the Italians and the Institutions who will be able to live alongside, in an atmosphere of mutual respect, with foreigners who know and follow the laws of the country where they found themselves.Coming to somebodys country without prior knowledge of what might come your way can be more frustrating than you ever imagined, in this one fees not wanted or hated by the Host country.The answer is simple just know few things before setting out on the journey.

Foreigners rights and duties

In Italy, every non European foreigner that is someone from a country outside the EU has the same fundamental human rights provided for by internal and international law (for example, a foreigner can freely defend his rights in a court the same way as any Italian citizen).

Instead, to practise civil rights (for example, the right to the National health services) the foreigner's status must be legally in order.

Every foreigner has the right to be able to contact the authorities of their own country, and the Italian public authorities are obliged to contact the nearest diplomatic or consulate representatives of the country which the foreigner comes from, informing them of any disciplinary action taken in the matter of personal freedom, removal from state territory, guardianship of minors, personal status, death or urgent hospital treatment.

The above is not valid in the case of refugees or persons seeking political asylum.

The President of the Council of Ministers prepares a programmatic document every 3 years which establishes the number of foreigners allowed, the criteria needed and the procedure to take, to enter State Territory.

A foreigner who is in State Territory and receives an income must observe all fiscal laws IV A (VAT) IRPEF (Personal Income Tax) or IRPEG (Corporation Tax) declarations etc.

The entrance and stay **of foreigners**

A) VISITORS VISA

The entrance into State Territory is permitted to foreigners with a valid passport (or any equivalent document) and an entrance visa.

All entrance visas can be obtained from the Italian diplomatic or consulate representatives in the foreigners country of origin. Together with the visa they will be given written documentation which explains their rights and obligations. The refusal of a visa may be contested in the ways prescribed.

A visa is granted if the foreigner can demonstrate that they are in possession of suitable documentation that confirms the purpose, housing conditions, means available to support them during their stay and for their return to tbeir country of origin. This last request is not necessary if the reason for their stay in Italy is to work

The visa is valid for not more than 90 days: to stay longer a Residence _permit_ is needed.

A visitors visa will be refused to those foreigners who must be those who have already been expelled.

For their family to accompany them, the foreigner must prove with appropriate Documentation, the family relationship or cohabitation. These documents must be shown at the Police Headquarters. It is also necessary to show availability of accommodation. The visa will be granted within 90 days of the request.

For visas that deal with the family joining them, the foreigner making the request must present the following documentation to the Police Headquarter demonstrating the particulars of the persons who wish to join them, they must also show

a) Residence papers b) Residence permit
c) Documents showing a regular income
d) Documents showing permanent accommodation.

When leaving State Territory, if the visitors visa has expired by not more than 60 days, the Foreigner must obtain a re-entry visa from the Italian diplomatic or consulate representative of their country of origin: They must also show the expired document.

The foreigner in possession of a visitors visa may re-enter Italy by showing the document and passport.

B) RESIDENCE PERMIT

If foreigners in possession of a Residence permit, Residence papers or other equivalent documents granted by the authorities of a state in the EU may stay in Italy.

A Residence permit must be applied for at the Police Headquarters of the Province, where the foreigner is, within eight working days of their entrance into State Territory.

The duration of the visa is variable, but it must not be longer than

a) Three months for business and tourist visas

b) Six months for seasonal work or nine months for seasonal work that needs more time.

c) A year, to study or attend an educational course (it can be re-new to give more time during the course.

d) Two years, for autonomous work, salaried work with an undetermined time limit or for family reasons.

e) If a foreigner needs a period of time relevant to their own special needs, they will be given specific documentation.

In order to request permission the foreigner must fill out the appropriate form predisposed by the Home Secretary. It must be signed by the applicant and be accompanied by four passport photos of the applicant.

In the request, the applicant must state their personal details, any young children (minors) who live with them, and who will therefore also be on their fathers permit, as well as where and the reasons why they are asking for a Residence permit.

As for Tourist permits, which last not more than 30 days, for guided groups, the request can be made by the group leader, by showing passports or equivalent documents.

For a short term permit to visit religious or civil communities, hospitals or other places of treatment, the request can be made by whoever presides over the structure where the foreigner is visiting.

To re-new a Residence permit the request must be presented in duplicate to the Police Headquarters at least 30 days before its expiry date.

The permit is renewable for a period of time that is not more than double that established on the initial permit.

It is not possible to re-new the permit if the foreigner has interrupted their stay   in Italy for a period of more than six months .(NOTE VERY IMPORTANT)

The Residence permit and it's renewal will be refused and, if already granted revoked, if the requested requirements needed to enter and stay in the State are not met.

The loss of their work place is not a reason to deprive a working foreigner and their legally resident family of a Residence permit.

The foreigner who is either provided with a Residence permit or an equivalent document granted by a State which is a member of the EU, must declare their presence to the Police Headquarters within eight working days of their entrance into State Territory: Where they will receive a receipt stating the declaration of their stay. Failure to do so will lead to a fine which ranges from euro 200,00 to euro 600,00 If within 60 days of their entrance into the country , he has not still declare their presence they may risk being expelled.

A Residence permit given for work both salaried or freelance, or for family reasons may be converted into a permit for one of the other reasons of consent.

A foreigner who is registered is obliged to renew, at their local council registry office, their declaration of residence, within 60 days of the renewal of the Residence permit, The aforementioned permit must be presented.

The Prefect can forbid foreigners from staying in areas or places which are of military interest to the state: Violation of this law can lead to them being removed by the Public Forces.

B) RESIDENCE PAPERS

When a foreigner has been in the Country for at least five consecutive years and they are in possession of a Residence permit which allows them an undetermined number of renewals they can ask for, themselves, their spouse and their children, a Residence paper from the Police Headquarters. .

The request has to be a certified copy approved by the Home Secretary. The request form asks for:

a) All personal details

b) Where they have been staying over the past 5 years

c) The place of residence

d) The amount of income and where it comes from

The request must be accompanied by:

a) A copy of their passport or other relevant document

b) A copy of their Tax return or a 10 1 form from the past year

c) Certificates showing any criminal records

d) Four passport photos or more

3   The Residence paper is issued within 99 days of the request and is valid for an undetermined amount of time. The paper must be endorsed by the applicant within 10 years of issue, and within 5 years of issue the paper is valid as a form of identification.

4 The request for the paper will be rejected if the foreigner has stood trial for one of the crimes listed in art. 380 c.p.p. (code of criminal procedure) (in cases of forced arrest during the process of committing the crime) or in art. 381 c.p.p. (code of criminal procedure) crimes for which they were not charged (in the case of voluntary arrest iri the process of committing the crime). The Papers will also be refused if the foreigner has been condemned for any of the above crimes, even if judgement was not passed. If the paper was issued before the said judgement the Police Headquarters are free to revoke it.

5 The holder of Residence papers can:

 a) enter State Territory without an entrance visa

 b) Set up any of the allowed activities, not those that are explicitly forbidden
    to foreigners

c) Obtain the services allocated by Public Administration

d) They can take part in local public life, they can also vote, as in conformity with the Convention of Strasburg 5 February 1992.

6 A holder of Residence papers can only be deported for serious crimes against public order or for reasons of National security.

7 One can contest refusal or revocation at the Tribunal Administrative Regional TAR (Regional Administrative Court).

D) ADMINISTRATIVE EXPULSION

For reasons of Public order or State security, the Home Secretary can order the expulsion of a foreigner, even if they are not resident in State Territory.

The Prefect can order expulsion when the foreigner

a) Entered State Territory without being checked by border officials .

b) Entered State Territory without applying for a Residence permit in the way prescribed or has had their permit revoked, annulled or it has expired for more than 60 days without a request for renewal being made.

c) Is a member of a category of people considered socially dangerous by the law.

3 The expulsion is carried out by the Police Headquarters with the help of the Public forces at the border when the foreigner:

a) Has unlawfully stayed longer than the time provided in State Territory.

b) Has already received the disciplinary action of expulsion, but there is a strong possibility they will try to avoid it.

4 The expulsion order consists of the ultimatum to leave State Territory within 15 days, the prescription for the journey and
   the documentation needed to present to the border police.

5 The expulsion decree- which must be translated into the foreigners own language, or if this is not possible, French,
   English or Spanish- is communicated to the party concerned.

6 To contest the decree, one can present an appeal to the Judge of the court which passed the expulsion within 5 days of its
   communication.

7 The Judge after hearing from the party concerned will make a decision within 10 days of

receiving the appeal.

8 The Appeal can even be presented through the Diplomatic representation or the Italian consulate in the destination state
  within 30 days of the disciplinary communication.

9 The foreigner has the right to free legal aid and if he does not have his own Defence lawyer the Judge will nominate one for him, and if necessary an interpreter.

10 To contest a decree of expulsion issued by the Home Secretary the appeal must be presented to the Regional Administrative Court in Lazio Tribunal Administrative Regional del Lazio TAR)

11 The deportee is sent to the country they arrived from or their country of origin.

12 The deportee can not return to State Territory for five years unless special permission is given by the Home Secretary, The Regional Administrative Court (TAR) or the Judge, after studying the appeal presented they will determine the period of time that the disciplinary action should last, however it cannot be for less than three years.

13 The Judge, in the case of sentence for one of the crimes mentioned earlier calls for articles 380 and 381 c.p.p. (code of criminal procedure) and if the foreigner is considered socially dangerous can issue a deportation order.

14 The Judge, trying a foreigner for a crime where the plea is not guilty or applying the sentence at the request of the accused according to art. 444 c.p.p. (code of criminal procedure) must consider giving a prison sentence of not more than two years, and if the sentence cannot be suspended, it can be substituted by expulsion for a period which is not less than five years.

15 Under no circumstances can the foreigner be deported or sent back to a country where they will be subject to persecution, for reasons of race, sex, language, citizenship, religion, political opinions or personal or social conditions.

16 Concession to expel foreigners
   a) under the age of eighteen
   b) in possession of Residence papers
   c) living with forth grade relatives or a spouse who is an Italian national
   d) who are pregnant, or whose children are not yet six months old - will not
   be given

E) DISCIPLINE AT WORK

1 The Loss of work place- even when one resigns- is not a reason to deny a working foreigner and their family legally resident a Residence permit. **In** the aforementioned case the foreigner can enrol at the labour exchange for the remainder of the time the permit is valid, however it must not be for less than one year.

2 Work permits for foreigners resident abroad are issued by the administrative offices of the province where they wish to work, at the request of their employer.

In the case of repatriation, a working foreigner will keep all social security rights they have accumulated.

They have the right to ask for a payment settlement of the contributions, higher than 5% annually, which have been paid in in their favour

The attributes of charitable institution and social assistance are available to

persons who are not EU *members,* but have regular work in Italy

Persons who are non ED members who work can participate in all information or educational courses in State Territory.

2   A different and more simplified procedure allows by law admittance into Italy for certain categories.

a) Management or specialized personnel with a branch or head office in Italy

b) University lecturers

c) Researchers or University Teachers d) Interpreters or Translators

e) Domestic Helps moving to Italy following Italian citizens when the job collaboration has been ongoing for at least one year.

f) Authorized personnel for professional training.

g) Labour depending on firms or organizations operating in Italy

h) Shipping labourers.

i) Foreign labourers waged abroad but working temporarily in Italy with put out contracts.

j) Circus or Travelling show entertainers

k) Artists or technicians working on shows, plays, concerts and ballets.

I) Dancers, Artists and musicians.

m) Sportsmen

n) Accredited journalists in Italy

0) Temporary live in workers.

Family unity rights

1. A foreigner in possession of a residence paper or permit valid for not less than one year, issued for salaried or freelance work, asylum, study or religious matters, has the right to maintain or re-establish his family unit.

2. In all the administrative or legal procedure regarding Family unity rights concerning minors, the interests of the minor is always highly regarded.

3. The foreigner can ask that the following family members join them: a) A spouse not legally separated

b) Parents who are dependent on them.

c) Children (minors) who are dependent on them and their spouse.

d) Up to third degree relatives who are dependent on them and unable to work according to Italian Law.

In these cases a foreigner must show that they have accommodation, as stated in the minimum requests of regional law.

The request for the family to rejoin them must be presented to the Questura (Police Headquarters).

After 90 days of making the request a foreigner can obtain the visa from the Italian diplomatic or consulate delegation.

It is also possible to request a residence permit for family reasons when:

a) A foreigner enters Italy with an entrance visa for the joining of the family.

b) A foreigner resident in Italy for one year, is married to an Italian citizen.

c) A relative to the foreigner is legally staying in Italy and has the necessary requirements for the family to join them.

d) A foreigner is the natural parent of an Italian minor living in Italy.

8 The Residence permit for family reasons allows:
Access to social assistance, the right to enrol to study or to take part in a training programme, enrolment to the employment list, and the carrying out of salaried or freelance work.

9   A foreigner joining an Italian citizen or another foreigner who is in possession of

residence papers is allowed papers themselves. .

10 To contest any disciplinary action from the Administrative Authority dealing   with family unity, the party concerned can appeal to the local court.

11 The decree permitting the claim allows for the issue of the Visa .

12 A foreigners child, who is a minor living with them, and who is legally staying in Italy is included on the permit or residence papers of one or both parents until the age of fourteen, and thereafter depending on Judicial conditions.

13 The Juvenile court in serious cases effecting the psychophysical development, and after taking into consideration the age and health conditions of the minor who is in Italy, can authorize entrance or family residence for an undetermined period of time, as a dispensation to Italian law.

14 The job of checking conditions of residence of foreign minors temporarily admitted in State Territory, is carried out by the Presidency of Council, an appropriate board.

Assistance from the NATIONAL HEALTH SERVICES

1. Foreigners are obliged to enrol in the National Health Service, under the same terms, conditions and rights as Italian citizens.

a) When they are legally resident in Italy and they are working in either salaried or freelance jobs, or they are enrolled on the employment list.

b) When they are legally resident in Italy and they have applied for a renewal of the title of residency under the terms dictated by the law.

2 Health Assistance is also due to any family members dependant on the legal resident.

3 The legally resident foreigner who does not enter into the categories mentioned, must insure themselves against illness, accidents and maternity, with insurance policies that are valid in National Territory.

4 Those foreigners who are legally resident in Italy for reasons of study or those working for board, can ask for a voluntary inscription to the National Health Service.

5 The above mentioned must pay a lump-sum contribution annually.

6 Foreigners who are not enrolled in the National Health Service must pay for the use of the Health service, the amount determined by the Region or Province.

7 Foreigners who are in Italy whose status has not been legalized, are assured that in hospitals or in outpatient departments they will be given the necessary treatment.

8 They are guaranteed:

a) Pregnancy and maternity treatments at tI;le same level of treatment received by Italian citizens.

b) Treatment for minors

c) The obligatory vaccinations or those given during a campaign for collective prevention

d) Operations for international prophylaxis.

e) The prophylaxis and the cure of infectious illnesses.

9 The admittance of a foreigner, whose- status has not been legalized, into a medical structure, does not mean them being reported to the public authorities, except in cases when referral is obligatory, as is the case with Italian citizens.

10 The foreigner, seeking medical cure in Italy, and if necessary the companion, can apply for a specific entrance visa along with its relevant Residency permit. The permit lasts as long as the treatment is necessary, and is renewable until treatment is finished.

Professional and educational activities

The foreigner who is legally resident in Italy and who holds a professional title legally recognised by the State, can apply for inscription the Professional Associations or colleges.

2 In the case of salaried work, they are guaranteed the same wage payments and social

security as Italian citizens.

3 Foreigners who are minors living in State Territory are obliged to attend school.

4 The Region and local authorities set up courses to aid the learning of the Italian language.

5 Scholastic institutions promote the setting up of Italian language courses as a cultural offer to foreign adults, and the availability of integrative courses on par with the studies carried out in their country of origin, so they may obtain a High school diploma.

6 In the matter of entrance into universities, equal treatment of foreign and Italian citizens is assured.

7 Every year the Minister for Foreign Affairs establishes the maximum number of entrance visas and residence permits to be issued, for reasons of university entrance to foreign students resident abroad.

8 Foreigners in possession of residence papers for salaried of freelance work or for family reasons, political or humanitarian asylum or religious reasons, can attend university courses, under the same terms as Italian students.

Hospitality and social assistance

The Region in collaboration with the provinces, the councils and voluntary associations predispose welcoming centres in order to accommodate foreigners, legally resident, who are finding it temporarily impossible to find housing or to maintain themselves.

2 The mayor can in situations of emergency, accommodate foreigners who are not of legal status in the welcoming centres.

3 A foreigner who is legally resident in Italy can enter dormitories, either public of private, in accordance with the law.   .

4 A foreigner who is the holder of Residency papers or is legally resident in Italy has the right to council housing on the same terms as any Italian citizen.

5   The foreigner who is in possession of Residence papers or has been legally resident in Italy for a duration of not less than one year has the same rights as Italian citizens to any help, even economical, to help from the social services, this includes those suffering from tuberculosis, the deaf and dumb, blind, disabled or destitute.

6 It is the job of the State, the Region, the provinces and the local councils to promote:

a) Enterprising activities for foreigners legally resident in Italy.

b) The circulation of any information that aids the integration of foreigners into society, especially anything regarding their rights and duties.

c) The charm of the cultural, recreational, social, economical and religious ways of foreigners legally resident.

d) The setting up of agreements with associations to find work for foreigners legally resident.

e) The organization of information courses which aid a peaceful cohabitation and help avoid discriminating or racist behaviour.

7   The Ministry of Ministers council, deals with any problems the foreigners or their family may have.

8 What constitutes discrimination:

Any behaviour, which directly or indirectly, involves a distinction, exclusion, restriction, or preference based on race, colour, ancestral national or ethnic origin, or creed, and which aims to destroy or to compromise the admission, the pleasure or practice. On equal terms with basic human rights and freedom, in the political, economical, social or cultural fields or any other sector of public life.It is always called constituted discrimination.

a) to omit acts which deal with the condition of foreigners only.

b) To force unjust conditions, which are not to one's advantage on the foreigner

c) To prevent or to obstruct the legitimate right of the foreigner to work.

d) If an employer carries out acts which lead to discriminatory action.

10 In the case of an act of discrimination the Judge can, at the request of the concerned party, order the cessation of the discriminating behaviour, and adopt any other appropriate procedure to end the act.

The petition can be made, also in person, by the concerned party through the registrar in the place where they are resident.

1 A foreigner who has been expelled, but nevertheless re-enters State Territory, will be imprisoned for 2 to 6 months after which they will be immediately expelled.

2 The employer who takes on foreigners without residence permits or whose permit has expired, been revoked or annulled will be punished with a fine. and a prison sentence of from 3 months to one year.

3 The same penalty applies to a employer who takes on a foreigner whose status is not legal, to carry out what is considered seasonal work.

4 In addition to these laws listed, all the laws of the penal code will also be in force.

10 In particularly articles 473 an d 474 of the penal code which carry a punishment of a fine of up to 2 mila euro and a prison sentence, the falsification of Industrial produce or inventions (imprisonment for up to 4 years), the falsification of audio or video cassette and their sale (imprisonment for up to 2 years).

I am putting on this small journal to guide old and new comer wanting to come to any European country to live and to serve as an eye opener to everybody especially in Italy where I live for decades.

In conclusion one could see that these countries do not HATE US if foreigner could follow the rules of their countries .

One can at thesme time call this journal or book an immigration guide to everyone.

m. james

www.ingramcontent.com/pod-product-compliance
Lightning Source LLC
Chambersburg PA
CBHW041304180526
45172CB00003B/959